Animals of North America
BIGHORN SHEEP

by Tammy Gagne

Caldwell County
Public Library
120 Hospital Ave • Lenoir, NC 28645

F⦵CUS
READERS

North Star
EDITIONS

www.northstareditions.com

Produced for North Star Editions by Red Line Editorial.

Photographs ©: Tom Reichner/Shutterstock Images, cover, 1; Kris Wiktor/ Shutterstock Images, 4–5; Red Line Editorial, 7; Greg and Jan Ritchie/ Shutterstock Images, 8–9; Chris Kolaczan/Shutterstock Images, 11; Lorraine Logan/Shutterstock Images, 12, 14–15; Wesley Aston/Shutterstock Images, 17; blewulis/iStockphoto, 18, 29; Michael Chatt/Shutterstock Images, 20–21; Beketoff Photography/Shutterstock Images, 22–23; James Marvin Phelps/Shutterstock Images, 25 (top); IPK Photography/Shutterstock Images, 25 (bottom right); Wildnerdpix/Shutterstock Images, 25 (bottom left), 26

ISBN
978-1-63517-032-0 (hardcover)
978-1-63517-088-7 (paperback)
978-1-63517-191-4 (ebook pdf)
978-1-63517-141-9 (hosted ebook)

Library of Congress Control Number: 2016951001

Printed in the United States of America
Mankato, MN
November, 2016

About the Author

Tammy Gagne has written more than 150 books for adults and children. She resides in northern New England with her husband and son. One of her favorite pastimes is visiting schools to talk to kids about the writing process.

TABLE OF CONTENTS

CHAPTER 1

ROCKY MOUNTAIN HOME

Bighorn sheep are wild **mammals** of North America. Many live in the Rocky Mountains. Some are found in southwestern Canada. Others live in the western United States.

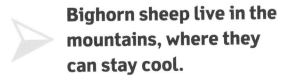

Bighorn sheep live in the mountains, where they can stay cool.

Bighorn sheep climb rocky cliffs as high as 8,500 feet (2,591 m) above sea level.

Bighorn sheep are also found in northern Mexico.

These strong animals can survive in the **alpine tundra** or in a desert climate. During summer, bighorn sheep seek out higher places in the mountains. The air is cooler at these higher **elevations**. When

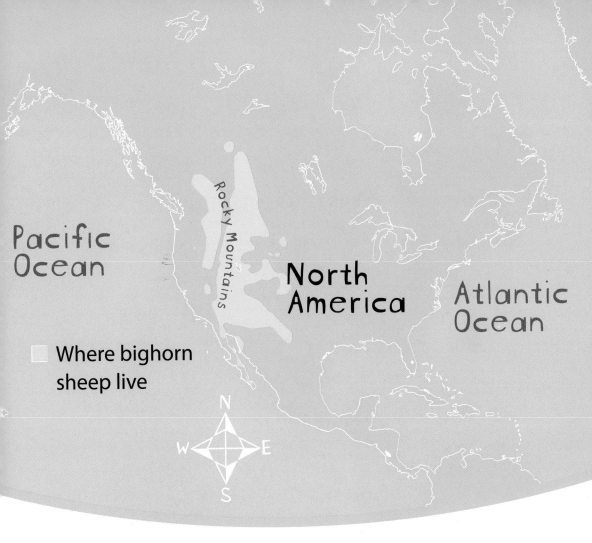

Pacific
Ocean

Rocky Mountains

North
America

Atlantic
Ocean

Where bighorn
sheep live

N
W E
S

> **Most bighorn sheep live along the
Rocky Mountain range.**

winter comes, bighorn sheep move

back to the warmer valleys.

CHAPTER 2

BIG AND STRONG

Bighorn sheep are named for their large horns. Male sheep are called rams. Ewes are female sheep. A ram's horns are longer than a ewe's. A ram's horns also curl much more than a ewe's.

A ram's horns can weigh as much as 30 pounds (14 kg).

An older ram's horns can be 3 feet (0.9 m) long from base to tip.

Bighorn sheep fur is short and mostly brown. The animal's **muzzle**, belly, and rump are white. In spring, the hair may look light gray. The animal sheds this winter coat. Darker fur grows in by summer.

FUN FACT

A ram's horns can weigh as much as all the other bones in its body combined.

Darker fur makes bighorn sheep harder to see against dark rocks and sand.

 Bighorn sheep stand approximately 3 feet (0.9 m) tall at the shoulders.

Bighorn sheep are the largest sheep in North America.

Bighorn sheep are very **muscular**. Most weigh 160 to 250 pounds (73 to 113 kg). Some rams weigh more than 350 pounds (159 kg).

CHAPTER 3

MADE FOR THE MOUNTAINS

Bighorn sheep have many traits that help them survive. They have excellent senses of smell and hearing. Their sharpest sense is their vision.

A bighorn sheep's eyes are far apart, allowing them to see a wide area.

Bighorn sheep's hooves help them stay on their feet while climbing and jumping. All of these senses help the sheep avoid **predators** such as mountain lions and wolves.

Bighorn sheep can stand on ledges only 2 inches (5.1 cm) wide. They can easily run and jump around mountains. Each hoof has

FUN FACT

Bighorn sheep can see other animals from 1 mile (1.6 km) away.

> Bighorn sheep often jump from one ledge to another.

a rough sole. This part grips rocks as the sheep walks over them. The animal's hooves are also split into two sections. This helps the sheep balance on uneven rocks and cliffs.

PARTS OF A BIGHORN SHEEP

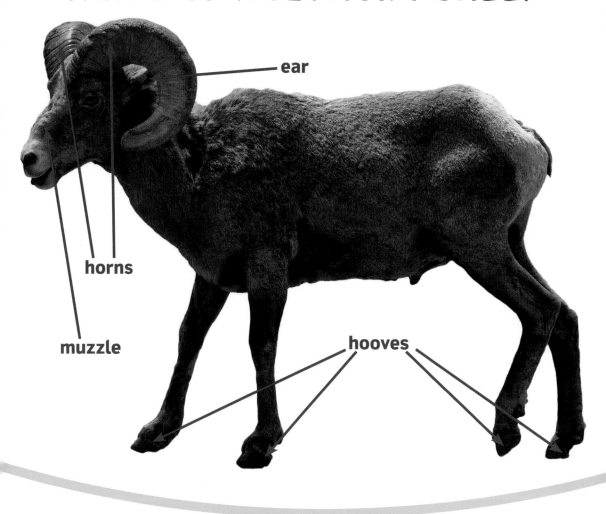

ear

horns

muzzle

hooves

One of the bighorn sheep's most
remarkable traits is its thick skull.
Rams need strong skulls to survive

all of the ramming they do. _____

often charge into each other with

their horns. These fights are usually

competitions for ewes.

Although they hit each other

hard, neither ram is seriously hurt.

The rams simply fight until one

gives up.

FUN FACT

Battles between rams can
last hours.

BUILT FOR BATTLE

How do rams butt heads without getting hurt? Their horns have many tiny holes. These holes are just big enough for air to pass through. The air acts as a soft cushion.

Ram horns can also bend a little when they are hit. This slight movement is a bit like an elastic band stretching. The stretching lessens the impact of each hit.

When one ram charges at another, it often reaches a speed of 40 miles per hour (64 km/h).

CHAPTER 4

LIFE IN THE HERD

Bighorn sheep live in groups called herds. Rams live in groups of two to five rams. Ewes live with other ewes and their lambs. A mother sheep usually has just one lamb.

Bighorn sheep are very social animals.

A young ram leaves its mother's herd when it is approximately two to four years old. During this time, the mother protects the young ram and teaches it how to survive. A young ewe stays with its mother's herd for life.

Bighorn sheep are **herbivores**. Their diet is made up of many plants. Bighorn sheep are diurnal. This means they are most active during the day. They spend most of each day eating.

BIGHORN SHEEP LIFE CYCLE

A ewe gives birth to just one lamb.

The lamb stays with its mother after birth and learns from her.

After approximately two to four years, the young rams leave their mothers' herds.

Bighorn sheep eat grasses, leaves, and twigs.

Because they live in such rocky areas, bighorn sheep do not have soft places to make their beds. They usually sleep on the bare ground. Most sheep spend nights near the top of a ridge. This location allows them to escape danger quickly.

FUN FACT

Bighorn sheep do not need to drink water during the winter. They get enough water from the plants they eat.

FOCUS ON
BIGHORN SHEEP

Write your answers on a separate piece of paper.

1. What do you think you were supposed to learn from reading this book?

2. Why do you think ewes have horns?

3. How many lambs does a ewe usually give birth to at one time?

    A. one

    B. two

    C. three

4. Why do bighorn sheep need to be able to move around rocky cliffs so well?

    A. Moving quickly across rocky cliffs helps the sheep see better.

    B. Moving quickly across rocky cliffs helps the sheep escape predators.

    C. Moving quickly across rocky cliffs helps the sheep hear better.

5. What does **sole** mean in this book?

    A. the bottom part of a foot

    B. one and only

    C. the spiritual part

Each hoof has a rough **sole**. This part grips rocks as the sheep walks over them.

6. What does **traits** mean in this book?

    A. horns

    B. herd members

    C. qualities

Bighorn sheep have many **traits** that help them survive. They have excellent senses of smell and hearing.

Answer key on page 32.

GLOSSARY

alpine tundra
A mountainous region in which trees do not grow.

elevations
Heights of land in relation to the sea.

herbivores
Animals that eat mostly plants.

mammals
Animals that give birth to live babies, have fur or hair, and produce milk.

muscular
Having a strong and powerful body.

muzzle
An animal's nose and mouth.

predators
Animals that kill and eat other animals.

TO LEARN MORE

BOOKS

Borgert-Spaniol, Megan. *Bighorn Sheep*. Minneapolis: Bellwether Media, 2016.

Gish, Melissa. *Bighorn Sheep*. Mankato, MN: Creative Education, 2016.

Lunis, Natalie. *Gravity-Defying Animals*. New York: Bearport Publishing, 2014.

NOTE TO EDUCATORS

Visit **www.focusreaders.com** to find lesson plans, activities, links, and other resources related to this title.

INDEX

Answer Key: 1. Answers will vary; **2.** Answers will vary; **3.** A; **4.** B; **5.** A; **6.** C